Guess WHO'S in the
BOOK OF MORMON

"For my own little heroes . . .
Jayden, Asher & Rhye"
—Molly

"Dedicated to Andrew, my husband, best
friend, and my favorite pillow all in one!"
—Katie

Text © 2018 Molly McNamara Carter
Illustrations © 2018 Katie Payne

This is not an official publication of The Church of Jesus Christ of Latter-day Saints. The opinions and views expressed herein belong solely to the author and do not necessarily represent the opinions or views of Cedar Fort, Inc. Permission for the use of sources, graphics, and photos is also solely the responsibility of the author.

ISBN 13: 978-1-4621-2197-7

Published by CFI, an imprint of Cedar Fort, Inc.
2373 W. 700 S., Springville, UT 84663
Distributed by Cedar Fort, Inc., www.cedarfort.com

Library of Congress Control Number: 2018936041

Cover design and typesetting by Katie Payne and Shawnda T. Craig
Cover design © 2018 Cedar Fort, Inc.
Edited by Kaitlin Barwick

Printed in the United States of America

10 9 8 7 6 5 4 3 2 1

Printed on acid-free paper

Guess WHO'S in the
BOOK OF MORMON

Written by Molly McNamara Carter

Illustrated by Katie Payne

CFI • An imprint of Cedar Fort, Inc.
Springville, Utah

Who built a boat and
sailed across the sea
and left a sacred record
for all the world to read?

NEPHI!

Yes, Nephi was the prophet
who built a great big boat.
He had the faith to
sail it, and on the plates
he wrote.

Who was the prophet who at first did not choose right, but when his father prayed for him, he changed and saw the light?

ALMA THE YOUNGER!

Yes, Alma the Younger was the prophet who used to preach against God's word. But then an angel came to him, and he shared what he had heard.

Who was the missionary who saved King Lamoni's sheep and taught him that when choosing good, great blessings he would reap?

AMMON!

Yes, Ammon was the missionary
who used his sword to fight.
He taught the wicked Lamanites to
repent and do what's right.

Who was the Lamanite woman who had learned the gospel long ago and waited until the time was right to let her great faith show?

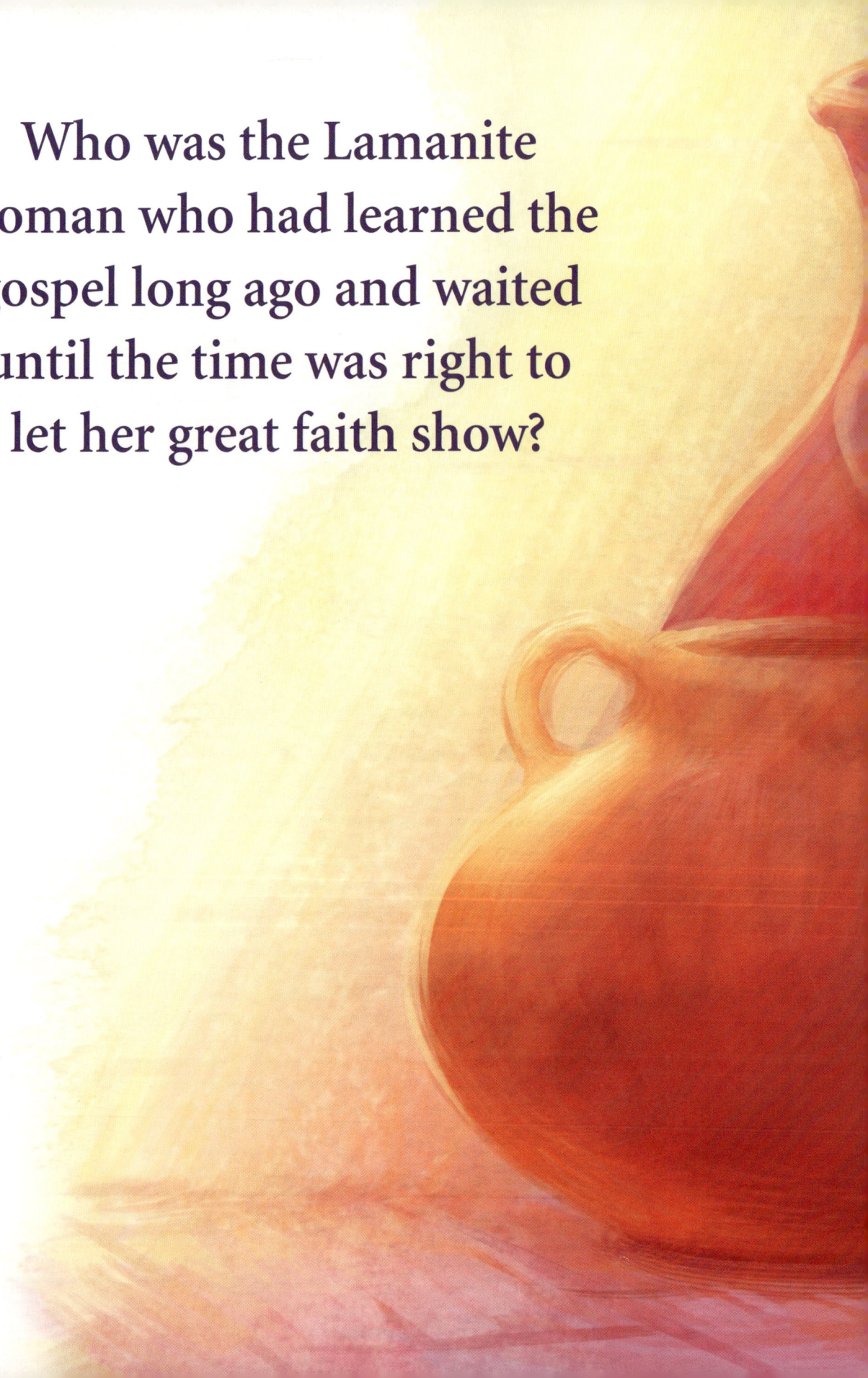

ABISH!

Yes, Abish was the woman who
was servant to a king. And when
she saw God's power shown,
the people she did bring.

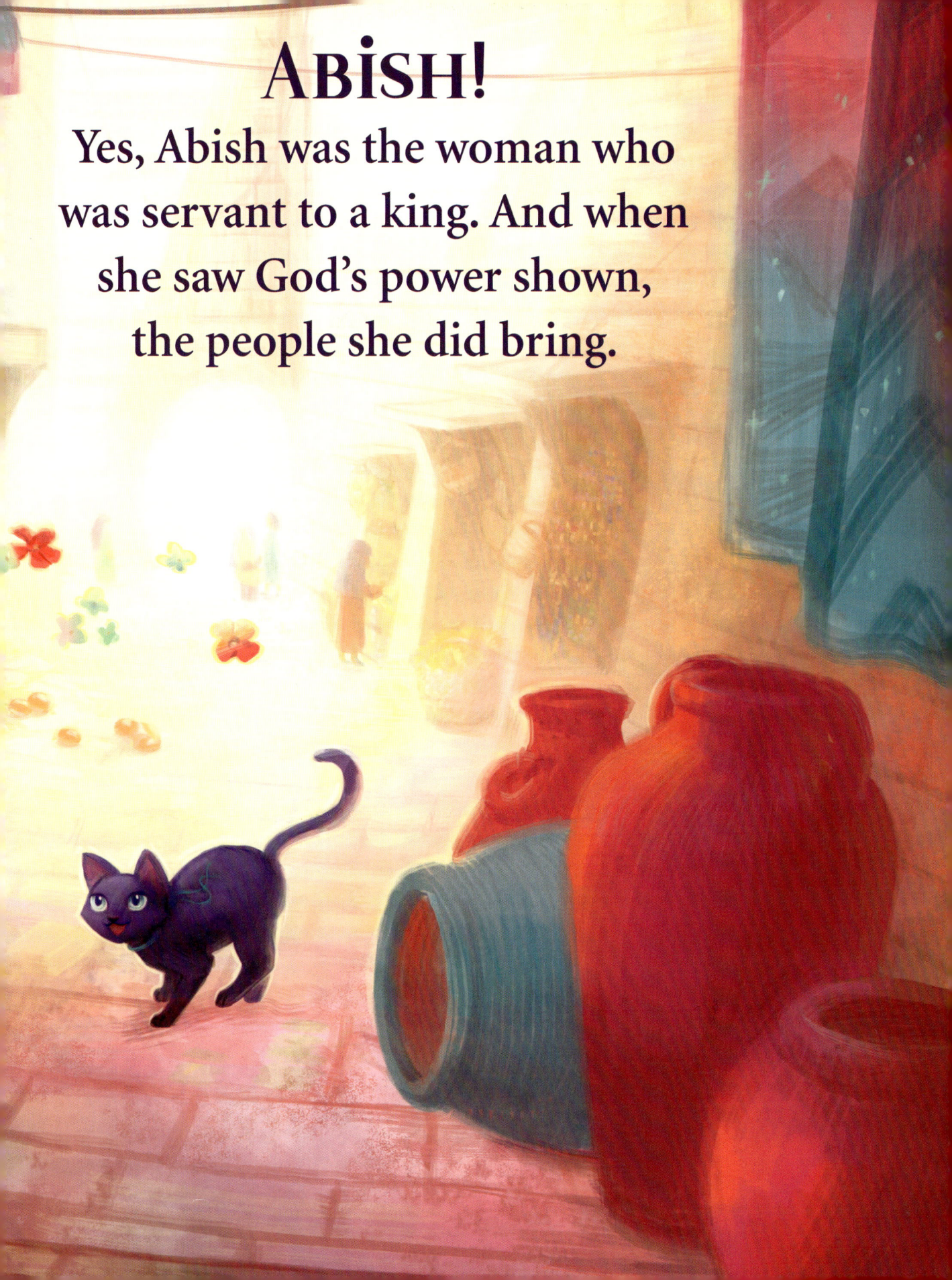

Who was the captain leading Nephites in a war? Freedom, peace, and family are what he told them to fight for.

MORONI!

Yes, Moroni was the captain who led against the foe. And with the title of liberty, into battle he did go.

Who climbed atop a city
wall in a stranger's land?
Who told the people
to repent and live
the gospel plan?

SAMUEL!

Yes, Samuel was the prophet
who told the Nephites to repent.
And after being turned back out,
to the wall he went.

Who was the leader long ago who compiled all the plates? Who wrote of many righteous men and told us of their fates?

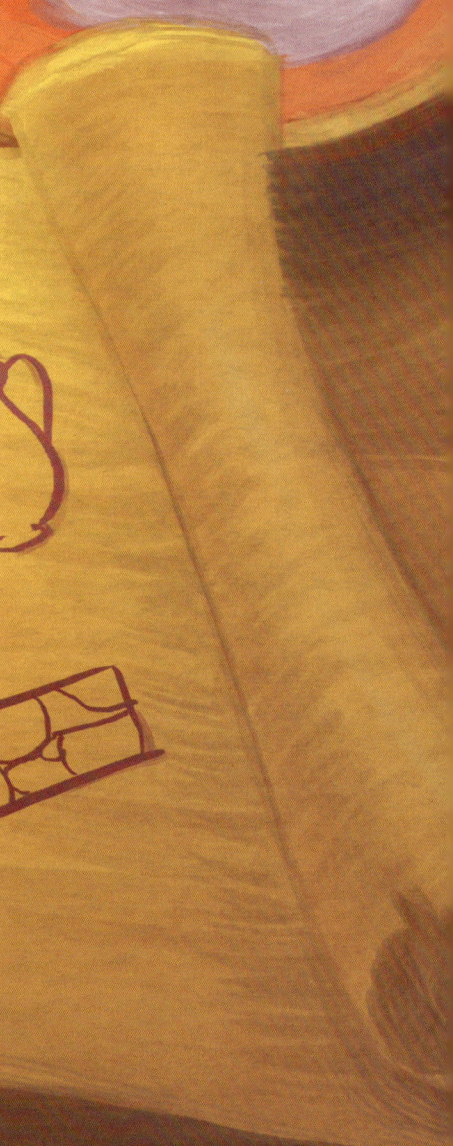

MORMON!

Yes, Mormon was the prophet who wrote with his own hand. He made for us this precious book with stories of his land.

In the Book of Mormon, these stories all are told, of these righteous people who lived in times of old.

They followed God's commandments and served each other well, and now we read their stories and of their faith we tell.